HIP-HOP DANCING

THE BASICS

VOLUME 1

by Wendy Garofoli

Consultant:
AleKsa "LeX" Chmiel, Co-Director/Owner
Flomotion Dance Company
Philadelphia, Pennsylvania

CAPSTONE PRESS
a capstone imprint

Velocity is published by Capstone Press,
151 Good Counsel Drive, P.O. Box 669, Mankato, Minnesota 56002.
www.capstonepub.com

Books published by Capstone Press are manufactured with paper
containing at least 10 percent post-consumer waste.

Library of Congress Cataloging-in-Publication Data
Garofoli, Wendy.
  Hip-hop dancing / by Wendy Garofoli.
    p. cm.
  Includes bibliographical references and index.
  Summary: "Provides step-by-step instructions for learning breaking, popping, locking,
and krumping hip-hop dance moves"—Provided by publisher.
  ISBN 978-1-4296-5484-5 (library binding)—ISBN 978-1-4296-5485-2 (library
binding)—ISBN 978-1-4296-5486-9 (library binding)—ISBN 978-1-4296-5487-6
(library binding)
  1. Hip-hop dance. I. Title.

  GV1796.H57G37 2011
  793.3—dc22   2010030394

Editorial Credits
Megan Peterson and Mandy Robbins, editors; Veronica Correia, designer; Marcie Spence,
    media researcher; Sarah Schuette, photo stylist; Karon Dubke, photographer;
    Laura Manthe, production specialist

Photo Credits
Capstone Studio: 25 (right), Karon Dubke, cover, 5, 7, 8–9, 10, 11, 12, 13, 14, 15, 16, 17,
18, 19, 20, 24, 26, 27, 28, 29, 30, 31, 32, 33 (top and bottom left), 34, 35, 36, 37, 38, 39,
40, 41, 42, 43, 44, TJ Thoraldson Digital Photography, 22, 23; Getty Images Inc.: Evan
Hurd Archive, 45; iStockphoto: alex_kz, 25 (left), chictype, 9 (right), Winiki, 9 (left); Library of Congress, 33 (bottom right); Shutterstock: alias (design element), Andrei Nekrassov,
4 (bottom left), averole (design element), kentoh (design element), lgorij, 6, Moguchev, 21
(bottom), Petrov Stanislav Eduardovich, 4 (background), Pokaz (design element), teacept, 21
(top), Yumanyan (design element).

Printed in the United States of America in Stevens Point, Wisconsin.
092010
005934WZS11

TABLE OF CONTENTS

FIRST THINGS FIRST

Hip-hop dance is one of the fastest-growing, most popular types of dance around. Most dance studios offer hip-hop dance classes. This funky dance style can also be seen in music videos, concerts, TV shows, and movies. If you want to learn how to dance hip-hop, it's best to start with the basics. But before you practice your first move, you'll need to learn that hip-hop dance includes many different styles.

Each hip-hop style has its own flavor. West Coast styles like popping and locking highlight sharp robotic ticks and **exaggerated** arm movements. Breaking, the East Coast classic, features swift footwork and acrobatic stunts. And the newer technique called krumping is an explosive style of self-expression. But there are a few things that all these styles have in common.

exaggerated—*performed in an over-the-top manner*

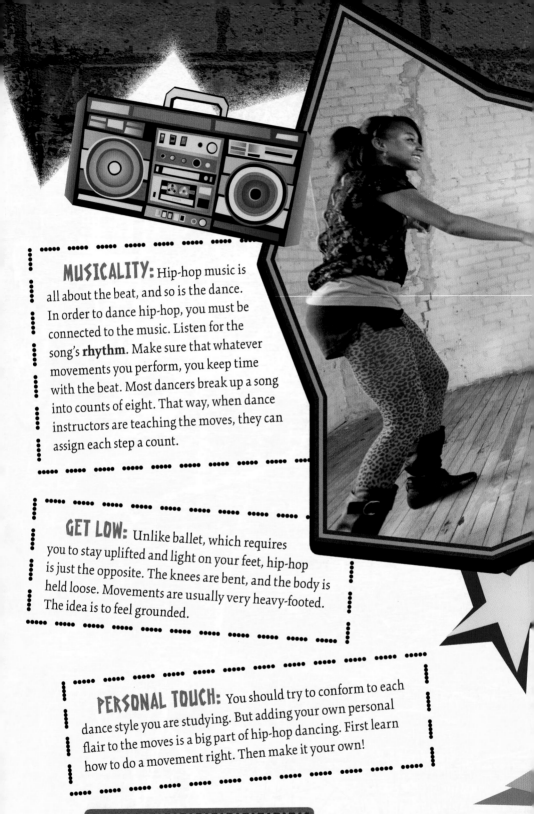

MUSICALITY: Hip-hop music is all about the beat, and so is the dance. In order to dance hip-hop, you must be connected to the music. Listen for the song's **rhythm**. Make sure that whatever movements you perform, you keep time with the beat. Most dancers break up a song into counts of eight. That way, when dance instructors are teaching the moves, they can assign each step a count.

GET LOW: Unlike ballet, which requires you to stay uplifted and light on your feet, hip-hop is just the opposite. The knees are bent, and the body is held loose. Movements are usually very heavy-footed. The idea is to feel grounded.

PERSONAL TOUCH: You should try to conform to each dance style you are studying. But adding your own personal flair to the moves is a big part of hip-hop dancing. First learn how to do a movement right. Then make it your own!

rhythm–*a regular beat in music or dance*

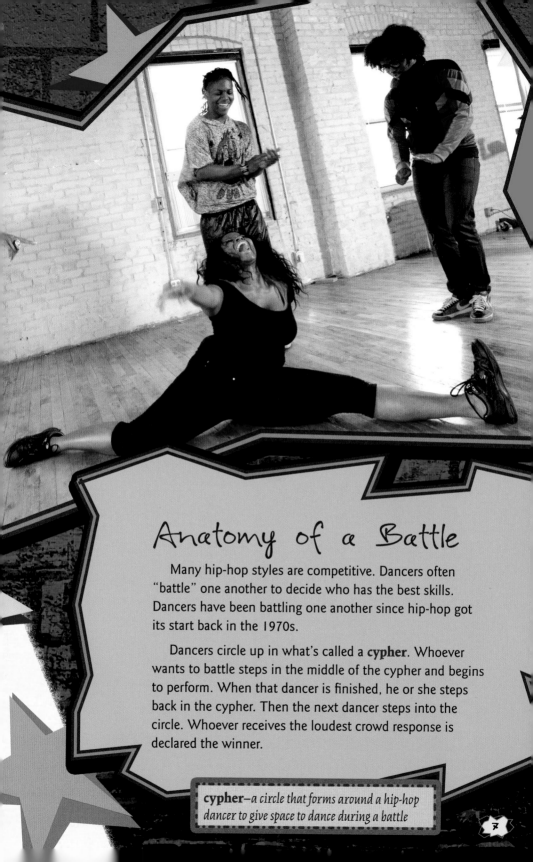

Anatomy of a Battle

Many hip-hop styles are competitive. Dancers often "battle" one another to decide who has the best skills. Dancers have been battling one another since hip-hop got its start back in the 1970s.

Dancers circle up in what's called a **cypher**. Whoever wants to battle steps in the middle of the cypher and begins to perform. When that dancer is finished, he or she steps back in the cypher. Then the next dancer steps into the circle. Whoever receives the loudest crowd response is declared the winner.

cypher–*a circle that forms around a hip-hop dancer to give space to dance during a battle*

STRETCHING

In hip-hop dance, you'll use almost all your muscle groups. You need to stretch them so you don't injure yourself while you dance. Move slowly as you stretch.

INNER THIGHS Sit on the ground in a **straddle** position. Reach forward to each toe to stretch your inner thighs.

BACK AND THIGHS Bend down and reach for your toes. This will stretch your back and the backs of your thighs.

ABDOMEN Bend your torso side-to-side to stretch your oblique muscles. These are the muscles on the sides of your abdomen.

NECK Tilt your head slowly to the right and left. Tilt your chin upward, and then slowly lower your chin into your chest.

WRISTS Roll your wrists around in circles clockwise and then counterclockwise.

Gear

Whether you practice in a studio or at home, you'll need the right gear to begin learning hip-hop:

- loose-fitting clothing, such as a T-shirt and sweatpants, to give you room to move
- sneakers with good support and grip to keep your feet from slipping
- kneepads to protect your knees during floor work

straddle — *a position in which a dancer is seated on the floor with the legs stretched out in a "V" shape*

LaTin Rock

DIFFICULTY: ☆

Inspired by salsa dancing, the **LATIN ROCK** is another fun and easy toprock move. Pop your hips as you perform this spicy step to the left and right.

Step 1

Stand with your feet close together. Cross your wrists at your waistline.

Step 2

Lift your left foot and take a wide step to the left. Pop your right hip as your foot touches the floor. As you do this, swing your arms to the left. Your arm movements should mirror your leg movements.

TiP

Although the Latin Rock stems from salsa, you'll want to make the hip and leg movements a bit stronger. Keep your hips slightly controlled. Stomp down hard with your feet.

Step 3

Step back to the starting position with arms crossed.

Step 4

Lift your right foot and take a wide step to the right. Repeat the opposite arm and hip position as in Step 2.

Step 5

Step back to the starting position. You can also perform the Latin Rock to the front and the back. Be sure to pop those hips!

Threading

DIFFICULTY: ★

THREADING is a basic floor work movement. When performed correctly, it looks like a dancer is tangling and untangling her legs at warp speed. Before you turn yourself into a human pretzel, here's an easy way to learn this move.

Step 1

Sit on the floor in a straddle position. Lean back with hands touching the floor.

Step 2

Prop up your right foot. Your right knee is bent, and your right foot is flat on the floor.

Step 3

Bend your left leg in and "thread" it under your right leg. Your right foot is crossed over your left leg. Your left leg is extended straight out in front of you.

Step 4

Lift your right leg. Sweep your left leg back to its starting position.

Step 5

You should end up back in the straddle position. To repeat the threading motion on the other side, prop up your left knee. Thread your right leg underneath your left leg.

Tip

Don't bring your foot in too close to your backside when you bend your knee. Leave enough space to slide your other leg underneath it.

C-C

The **C-C** is a **transition** step that is often performed between quick-stepping floor work movements. It involves a swift twist of the body and flick of the legs as you lean to each side. The C-C is a great way to learn how to shift your weight when breaking on the ground. It also strengthens your arms for more difficult steps to come.

Step 2

Extend your right leg straight in front of you with the right heel resting on the ground. Lean slightly over to the right side.

Step 1

Begin in a squatting position with your heels raised and your arms by your sides. Keep the fingers lifted instead of letting the palm lie flat on the ground. Be sure not to lean too far forward in the squat. Instead, keep your back straight and your stomach tight.

transition—*a step performed in order to move from one dance step to another*

Step 3

Reach your left hand across your body and touch the ground next to your right hand. As you do so, your entire body will twist to the right.

Step 4

Tuck your left knee next to your right knee. Keep it bent as you twist over. Your left foot will lift off the ground. Your right leg remains straight.

Step 5

As you twist over, kick your left foot into the air. Then untwist your body and return to the position in Step 2. Don't let your hips sink. Tuck your right leg back into the squatting position. Repeat the C-C to the other side by extending your left leg and twisting to the left.

TiP

Perform a Double C-C by twisting to each side twice. First twist to the right, and then return to the position in Step 2. But don't reset in the squat. Instead, lean back over to the right and twist again.

Six-Step

DIFFICULTY: ★☆

Just as its name suggests, the **SIX-STEP** is a floor work move that is completed in six steps. In this move, all parts of the body are at work as you rotate in a circle on the floor. The Six-Step is considered the foundation move for breaking floor work.

Step 1

Position your body as if you are starting a push-up. Hold your stomach tight and your back straight. Keep your neck straight by looking at the floor.

Step 2

Step forward with your left leg, aiming for your right hand. At the same time, pick up your right hand. Your left leg is crossed in front of your right leg.

Step 3

Bring your right foot forward and tuck it under your left ankle. Both knees are bent. Your right foot supports most of your body weight.

Step 4

Lift your left foot, uncross your ankles, and sit in a squat position. As you do this, your body will lift up. Both of your hands will be free and waiting by your sides.

Step 5

Drop your right hand to the ground directly next to your hip. At the same time, cross your right foot over your left foot. You are in the opposite position as you were in Step 3.

continued on next page

Six-Step

Step 6

Keep your left hand lifted and your right foot planted. Step back with your left foot. Your body should look like a mirror image of your position in step 2.

To complete the Six-Step, place your left hand back on the floor and step with your right foot back into a push-up position. You can continue to rotate around in six steps for as long as you like. Once you get the hang of leading with the left leg, try the Six-Step starting with your right leg.

Break Beats

Many pioneering b-boys and b-girls got their start by dancing to break beats. Break beats are the "breakdown" part of a song where the beat of the music is highlighted. DJ Clive "Kool Herc" Campbell introduced the break beat in the early 1970s. Herc would fast-forward his records to the instrumental part of a song and play it over and over again. The dancers at his parties couldn't help but head out to the dance floor. In fact, the "B" in b-boy and b-girl actually stands for "break."

TiP Most b-boys and b-girls don't drop to a push-up position in the middle of a battle to start the Six-Step. Instead, they perform a leg sweep into Step 5 and then rotate around.

POPPING MOVES

Neck Pops

DIFFICULTY: ⭐

NECK POPS are an important first step in popping. They **isolate** the neck muscles in order to push the head forward, backward, and side-to-side. While performing Neck Pops, a dancer's head appears to float off his or her body!

Step 1

Stand in a relaxed position. Without tilting the head up or down, push your chin forward as far as you can comfortably go.

Step 2

Bring your head back to center. Pull your chin into your neck without tilting your head up or down. Try to make a double chin.

isolate—to highlight a particular muscle or area of the body

Step 3

Bring your head back to the center. Push your head as far to the right as possible without tilting. Imagine pressing your right cheek up against a wall that is a few feet away from you.

Step 4

Bring your head back to center, and then push your head to the left.

TiP

When performing Neck Pops, focus more on tightening than relaxing the muscles. And don't forget to stretch your neck muscles before you attempt this move.

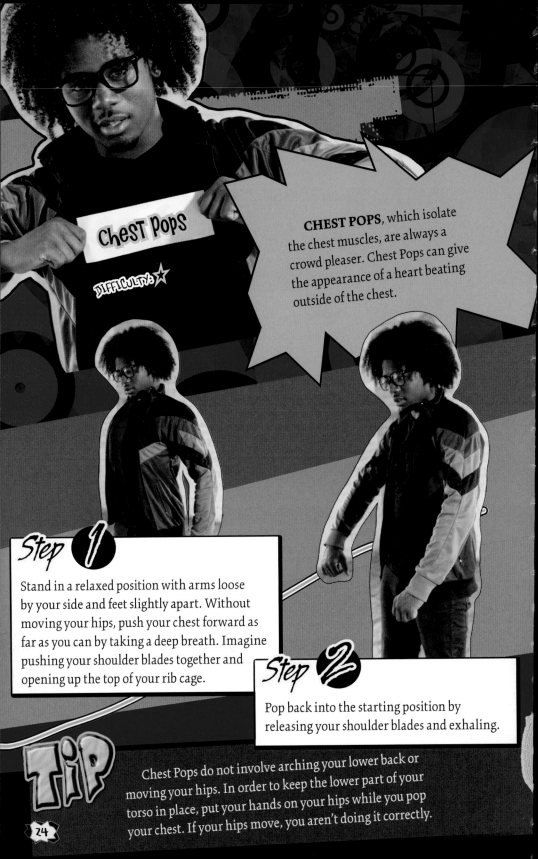

Chest Pops

DIFFICULTY: ⭐

CHEST POPS, which isolate the chest muscles, are always a crowd pleaser. Chest Pops can give the appearance of a heart beating outside of the chest.

Step 1

Stand in a relaxed position with arms loose by your side and feet slightly apart. Without moving your hips, push your chest forward as far as you can by taking a deep breath. Imagine pushing your shoulder blades together and opening up the top of your rib cage.

Step 2

Pop back into the starting position by releasing your shoulder blades and exhaling.

Tip

Chest Pops do not involve arching your lower back or moving your hips. In order to keep the lower part of your torso in place, put your hands on your hips while you pop your chest. If your hips move, you aren't doing it correctly.

Popping and Locking 411

Popping is sometimes incorrectly called "Poplocking." In reality, popping and locking are two separate dance styles with their own moves and costumes. They are both considered funk styles, an umbrella term for many hip-hop dance styles developed on the West Coast.

	Popping	Locking
history	created by Sam "Boogaloo Sam" Solomon in the mid-1970s	created by Don Campbell in the late 1960s
movements	sharp ticks of the muscles	bold, playful movements
costumes	large pinstriped suits	bright, colorful clothing; striped knee socks, suspenders
music	funk music of the 1960s, 1970s, and 1980s, including James Brown, Rick James, and Afrika Bambaataa; any hard-hitting hip-hop music of today	

James Brown
PAPA'S GOT A BRAND NEW BAG

Arm Wave

DIFFICULTY ★★★☆☆

The **ARM WAVE** is a combination of tiny isolated ticks in the knuckles, wrists, elbows, and shoulders. First master each tick. Then string them together to create the illusion that a wave is passing through your arms.

Step 1

Raise your right arm to the side at shoulder level. Your palm and fingers should be parallel to the floor.

Step 2

Bend your wrist up to a flexed position and bend your fingers down at the center finger joints.

Tip

To master the Arm Wave, practice each tick slowly. As you become more familiar with each tick, you can move from one position to the next more quickly. Finally, you will move so quickly that the audience won't see each individual tick. Instead, they'll be amazed by your smooth wave.

Step 3

Bend fingers down at the knuckles.

Step 4

Bend your hand down at the wrist, keeping your hand flat. Your fingers should now point straight down to the floor.

Step 5

Bend your arm at the elbow and lift the elbow to shoulder height. At the same time, flex your wrist so the palm is parallel to the floor.

Step 6

Straighten your elbow and lift your shoulder toward your ear at the same time. Now you have completed waving in. To wave out to the other side, release the right shoulder. Lift the left shoulder and repeat steps 1-5 in reverse.

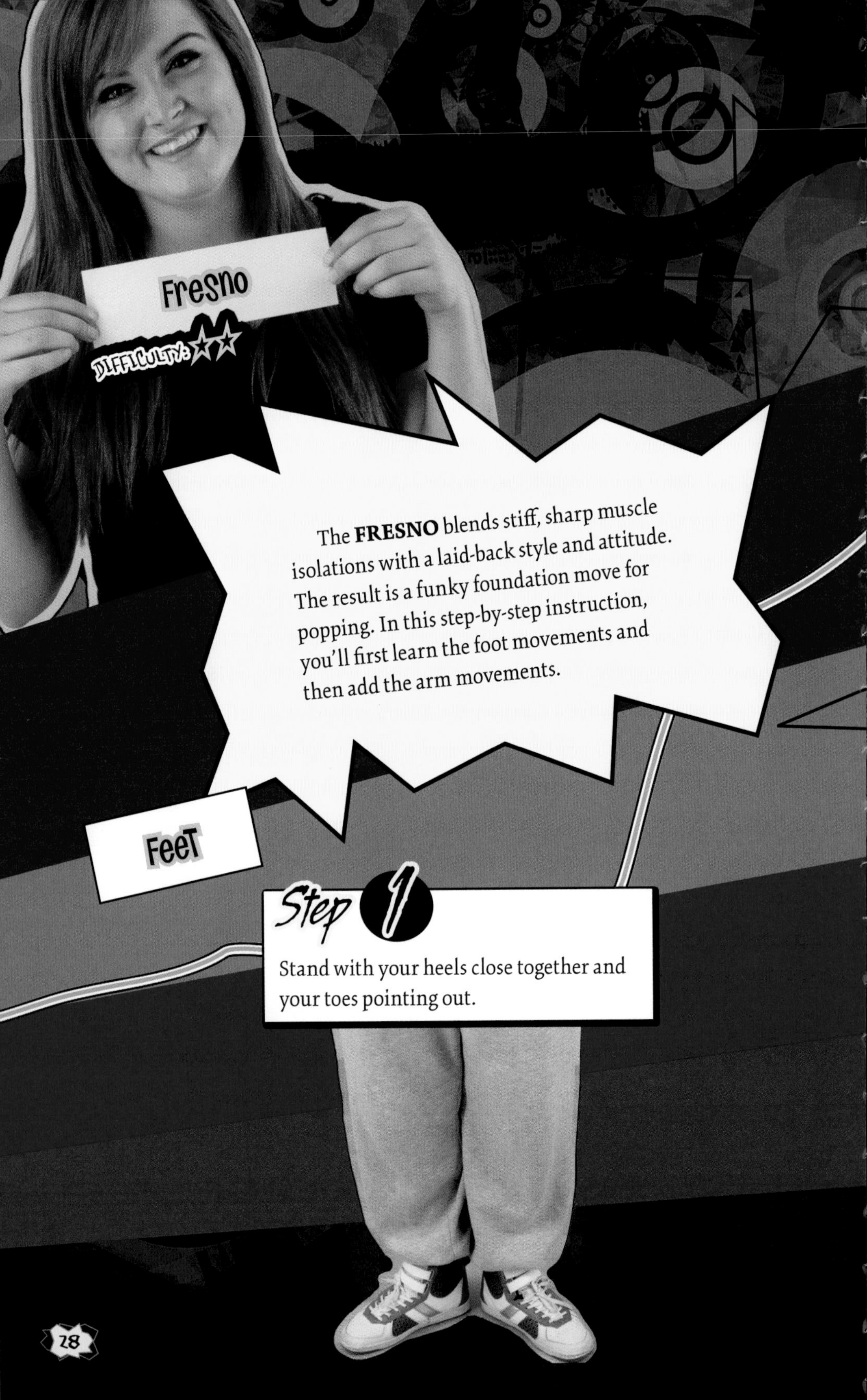

Fresno

DIFFICULTY: ★ ★

The **FRESNO** blends stiff, sharp muscle isolations with a laid-back style and attitude. The result is a funky foundation move for popping. In this step-by-step instruction, you'll first learn the foot movements and then add the arm movements.

FeeT

Step **1**

Stand with your heels close together and your toes pointing out.

Step 2

Slide your right heel and rotate your foot so that it is parallel to your left foot. Your left foot stays in the same position. As your right heel stops, pop the leg by tightening the muscles in your thigh.

Step 3

Bring your feet back to the starting position.

Step 4

Repeat the motion to the left, sliding the left heel and popping the left leg.

continued on next page

Fresno Arms

Step 1

Now you can add the arms. Keep your arms down at your sides in the starting position.

Step 2

As you slide your right heel, begin to lift your right arm straight out in front of you. As you pop your right leg, pop your right arm by tightening just the bicep muscle in your upper arm.

Step 3

Drop the arm as your feet return to the starting position.

Step 4

Repeat the arm movements to the left.

TIP

The Fresno's starting position takes up only half a count (AND). Your arm and leg pops take two counts (1-2). The move goes AND-1-2 (to the right) AND 3-4 (to the left). You can rock back and forth for as many counts as you like.

Chapter 3

LOCKING MOVES

Uncle Sam Points

DIFFICULTY: ★

UNCLE SAM POINTS were actually named after a famous World War I (1914–1918) poster featuring Uncle Sam. Uncle Sam is a character that stands for the U.S. government. In the poster, Uncle Sam points at whoever looks at the poster. And that's just what you'll be doing—playfully pointing at your audience!

Step 1

Stand in a relaxed position with both arms down at your sides.

Step 2

Extend your left arm straight out at the shoulder.

Step 3

Drop your left arm back to your side. Repeat steps 2-3 to the right.

TiP

Adding your own personal style to Uncle Sam Points is a key part of the move. You can point in any direction, including to the front or across your body. You can even point with both arms at the same time.

The Lock

DIFFICULTY: ☆

THE LOCK is one of the most important moves in locking. It requires you to hit a position and lock into place by tightening the muscles in your body. Then you relax the muscles and move on to the next step.

Step 1

Stand with your feet together and arms by your sides. Lift your right heel and bend both knees. Point the right knee away from the left leg, making a diamond shape. At the same time, bend forward and hunch your shoulders.

Tip

You should feel the muscles in your arms tighten as you lift them in step 3. If you don't feel a strain in your muscles, then you aren't doing the move correctly. Be sure to hold the position for a beat in order to give the move the "lock" effect.

Step 2

As you bend your knees and hunch forward, lift your arms, bending them at the elbows. Your elbows should be pushed forward so that they are almost in line with your shoulders. Lock your arms into place.

Step 3

Release the position by relaxing the arms, dropping the heel, and standing straight up again.

Good Times

Locking can be a comical dance style. Its dancers have fun interacting with the audience. Whether performing on a stage or in a club, lockers often head into the crowd. They give members of the crowd high fives. They even pull aside audience members to dance with them.

Scuba Hop

DIFFICULTY: ★★

The **SCUBA HOP** involves a little bit of kicking, a little bit of hopping, and a whole lot of fun. The trick is to switch feet quickly enough so that you don't balance on one leg for too long.

Step 1

Stand in a relaxed position with feet together. Lift your left knee to waist height.

Step 2

Extend your left leg straight out to the left. Keep the toes of your left foot facing forward.

Step 3

Swing your left leg straight down and hop onto your left foot. As your left foot lands on the floor, swing your right leg to the right. You should land with your right leg extended to the side and the right toes facing forward.

Step 4

Lift your right knee to waist height. Jump up, pushing off with your left foot. As you jump, bend the left knee as well. Land first with your right foot slightly behind you. Then land with your left foot slightly in front of you. Do not land with both feet at the same time!

Tip

Be sure to start and land any jump with your knees bent. Landing with straight knees puts too much pressure on your knees and could result in injury.

Stop'n Go

DIFFICULTY: ★★☆

The **STOP 'N GO** is a fun, bouncy move. It involves keeping track of arms and legs and changing directions. Once you get the hang of it, you won't want to stop!

Step 1

Stand with feet together. Bend your elbows and raise your hands to about shoulder height. Mimic the position you'd take if you were making a muscle in both arms.

Step 2

Step back with your right foot. At the same time, punch your right arm toward your left foot. You should be leaning slightly forward.

Step 3

Turn your body to the right. Release your right arm and point your left thumb at your chest. Your weight is mostly on your right leg. Your left leg is extended toward the front of the room.

Step 4

Swing back around to the same position as in Step 2.

Step 5

Step back to the starting position with both arms raised.

TIP

Perform the Stop 'n Go to songs by soul master James Brown. Lockers love dancing to his funky tunes for their upbeat, party vibe.

Chapter 4

KRUMPING MOVES

Arm Swings

DIFFICULTY: ★

ARM SWINGS are a fundamental move for krumping. They can be pulled off in a number of different ways. But they are always performed in a forceful manner. The more energy you put into your Arm Swings, the better they will look.

Snatch

Step 1

Whip your right or left arm down as hard as you can.

Step 2

Pull back the arm quickly so that it looks like you are snatching something away from someone.

40

Jerk

Step ❶

Jerk your body back as though you have whiplash. As you jerk your body, raise your right arm.

Step ❷

Throw down your right arm forcefully.

continued on next page

Drag

Step 1

Extend your right arm to the side. Twist your body back to the right as if you are winding up to throw a baseball.

Step 2

Drag the arm through the air as you twist your body back to the front. Delay the move a bit before you release and throw the arm down.

STomps

Krumpers use **STOMPS** to keep time with the music. Between other movements, they pound their feet on the floor to the beat of the song.

Step 1

Stand with your feet shoulder-width apart. Kick your right foot to the right. Keep the foot flexed.

Step 2

Bend your right knee and lift the leg. Your right foot should be about as high as your left knee.

Step 3

Stomp down on the floor with a flat foot as hard as you can.

TiP

Krumping is performed to hip-hop music with a slower beat and a gritty sound. Try listening to songs by rapper Missy Elliott and krumping pioneer Tight Eyez while practicing your Stomps.

Buck Hop

DIFFICULTY: ★

Krumpers don't just stand in place, stomp their feet, and throw their arms. They move across the floor using moves called travels. One of the more basic and important travels is the **BUCK HOP**. It pumps up the dancer to an even higher level of energy.

Step 1

Stand with feet shoulder-width apart. Hop to the right, jumping off the left foot. Keep your knees bent and feet flexed.

Step 2

Land first with your right foot.

Step 3

Stomp down with your left foot. You can travel to the other side by jumping off your right foot and hopping to the left. This time, land with your left foot first and then touch down with your right.

TIP

For even more emphasis, jump up and stomp both feet.

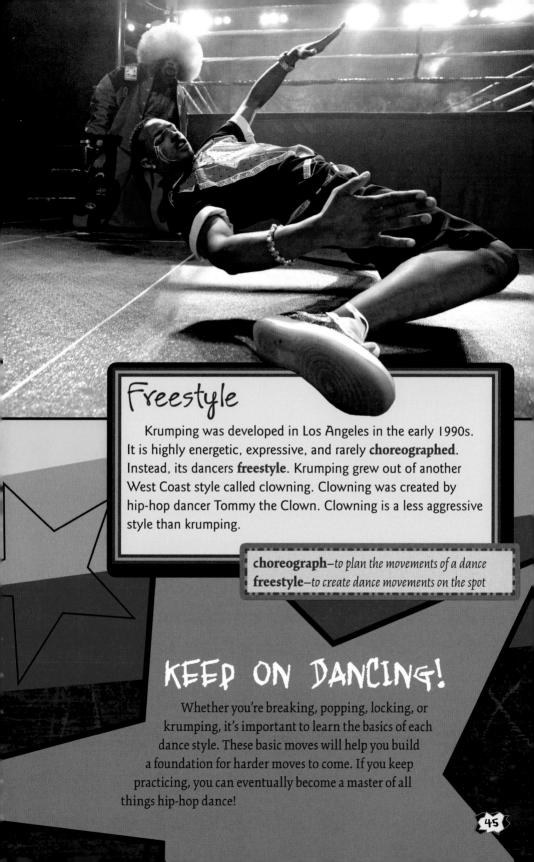

Freestyle

Krumping was developed in Los Angeles in the early 1990s. It is highly energetic, expressive, and rarely **choreographed**. Instead, its dancers **freestyle**. Krumping grew out of another West Coast style called clowning. Clowning was created by hip-hop dancer Tommy the Clown. Clowning is a less aggressive style than krumping.

choreograph—*to plan the movements of a dance*
freestyle—*to create dance movements on the spot*

KEEP ON DANCING!

Whether you're breaking, popping, locking, or krumping, it's important to learn the basics of each dance style. These basic moves will help you build a foundation for harder moves to come. If you keep practicing, you can eventually become a master of all things hip-hop dance!

GLOSSARY

battle (BAT-uhl)—a competition between individual dancers or groups; the dancers who receive the loudest crowd applause win

choreograph (KOR-ee-oh-graf)—to design or plan the movements of a dance

cypher (SY-fuhr)—a circle that forms around a breaker to give space to dance during a battle

exaggerated (eg-ZAA-jur-ay-ted)—something that seems bigger, better, and more important

freestyle (FREE-styl)—to create dance movements on the spot

isolate (EYE-suh-late)—to highlight a particular muscle or area of the body separate from the others

rhythm (RITH-uhm)—a regular beat in music or dance

rotate (ROH-tate)—to turn in a circle around a center point

salsa (SAHL-suh)—a popular style of music and dance that originated in Puerto Rico

straddle (STRAD-uhl)—a position in which a dancer is seated on the floor with his or her legs stretched out in a "V" shape

transition (tran-ZISH-uhn)—a step performed in order to move from one dance step to another

READ MORE

Cornish, Melanie J. *The History of Hip Hop.* Crabtree
Contact. New York: Crabtree Pub., 2009.

Fitzgerald, Tamsin. *Hip-Hop and Urban Dance.* Dance.
Chicago: Heinemann Library, 2009.

Freese, Joan. *Hip-Hop Dancing.* Dance. Mankato, Minn.:
Capstone Press, 2008.

Garofoli, Wendy. *Hip-Hop Dancing Volume 2: Breaking.*
Hip-Hop Dancing. Mankato, Minn.: Capstone Press, 2011.

INTERNET SITES

FactHound offers a safe, fun way to find Internet sites
related to this book. All of the sites on FactHound have
been researched by our staff.

Here's all you do:

Visit *www.facthound.com*

Type in this code: 9781429654845

INDEX